W9-AMN-769

Eco

Inventions and Discoveries

Economics

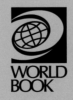

WORLD BOOK

a Scott Fetzer company

Chicago

www.worldbookonline.com

World Book, Inc.
233 N. Michigan Avenue
Chicago, IL 60601
U.S.A.

For information about other World Book publications, visit our Web site at **http://www.worldbookonline.com** or call **1-800-WORLDBK (967-5325)**.
For information about sales to schools and libraries, call **1-800-975-3250 (United States)**, or **1-800-837-5365 (Canada)**.

Editorial:
Editor in Chief: Paul A. Kobasa
Project Managers: Cassie Mayer, Michael Noren
Editor: Brian Johnson
Researcher: Cheryl Graham
Content Development: Odyssey Books
Writer: Cheryl Reifsnyder
Manager, Contracts & Compliance
  (Rights & Permissions): Loranne K. Shields
Indexer: David Pofelski

Graphics and Design:
Associate Director: Sandra M. Dyrlund
Manager: Tom Evans
Coordinator, Design Development and Production:
  Brenda B. Tropinski
Contributing Designer: Adam Weiskind
Contributing Photographs Editor: Carol Parden
Senior Cartographer: John M. Rejba

Pre-Press and Manufacturing:
Director: Carma Fazio
Manufacturing Manager: Steven K. Hueppchen
Production/Technology Manager: Anne Fritzinger

Library of Congress Cataloging-in-Publication Data

Economics.
    p. cm. -- (Inventions and discoveries)
  Includes index.
  Summary: "An exploration of the transformative impact of inventions and discoveries in the field of economics. Features include fact boxes, sidebars, biographies, and a timeline, glossary, list of recommended reading and Web sites, and index"--Provided by publisher.
  ISBN 978-0-7166-0392-4
  1. Economics--Juvenile literature. 2. Economic history--Juvenile literature.
3. Inventions--Juvenile literature. I. World Book, Inc.
HB183.E262 2009
330--dc22
                    2008042563

Picture Acknowledgments:
Front Cover: © Frances Roberts, Alamy Images.
Back Cover: © The Print Collector/Alamy Images.

© Ambient Images, Inc./Alamy Images 17, 44; © Blickwinkel, Alamy Images 33; © David R. Frazier Photolibrary/Alamy Images 11; © Horizon International Images Ltd./Alamy Images 23; © Michael Klinec, Alamy Images 43; © Art Kowalsky, Alamy Images 4; © Richard Levine, Alamy Images 33; © LOOK die Bildagentur der Fotografen/Alamy Images 39; © Dennis MacDonald, Alamy Images 13; © The Print Collector/Alamy Images 12; © Fredrik Renander, Alamy Images 42; © David Young-Wolff, Alamy Images 26; © American Express 27; AP Wide World 30; Art Resource 4, 6; © Erich Lessing, Art Resource 4; © Reunion des Musees Nationaux, Art Resource 8, 9, 19, 36; © Scala/Art Resource 10; © Bridgeman Art Library 4, 5; © Ariel Skelley, Blend Images/Digital Railroad 15; © Federal Reserve Bank of New York 20; © Steve Krongard, Getty Images 29; © Spencer Platt, Getty Images 17; © Don Smetzer, Getty Images 25; Granger Collection 16, 17, 18, 22, 24, 25, 34, 37, 38, 40, 41; © Tim Shaffer, Reuters/Landov 22; Mary Evans Picture Library 19, 39; © NCR 28; Shutterstock 7, 14, 18, 27, 29, 31, 32, 44; © SuperStock 31; Tropinski Family Archive 23.

All maps and illustrations are the exclusive property of World Book, Inc.

Inventions and Discoveries
Set ISBN: 978-0-7166-0380-1
Printed in China
1 2 3 4 5 12 11 10 09

▶ Table of Contents

There is a glossary of terms on pages 45-46. Terms defined in the glossary are in type **that looks like this** on their first appearance on any spread (two facing pages).

► Introduction

Throughout history, people have traded goods and services.

What is an invention?

An invention is a new device, new product, or new way of doing something. Inventions change the way people live. Before the car was invented, some people rode horses to travel long distances. Before the light bulb was invented, people used candles and similar sources of light to see at night. Today, inventions continue to change the way we live.

What is economics?

An economy is a system in which people exchange goods and services with other people. Goods include items like food, clothing, bicycles, and computers. Services include things like house cleaning, haircuts, and health care. An economy involves buyers, sellers, workers, and employers.

Businesses, governments, and various other organizations play important roles in economies.

Over thousands of years, people have developed many different types of economies, and each has its own rules. The study of economies is called economics. People who study economics are called economists.

Ancient people invented economic tools we now take for granted, such as coins.

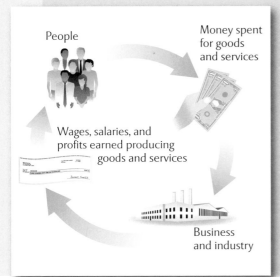

People

Money spent for goods and services

Wages, salaries, and profits earned producing goods and services

Business and industry

People

Labor and skill provided to business and industry

Goods and services purchased

Business and industry

The distribution of money, goods, and services makes up the pattern of a typical economy.

A country's economy is made up of money that flows from individuals to businesses and back again. People buy goods and services, providing money to businesses. Businesses give money back to individuals as **wages** and **salaries.** Many factors influence this flow of money, including the availability of workers and resources, people's desire for certain goods, and the setting of prices. Governments can influence an economy by managing the amount of money available and by making laws to regulate (control) the trade of goods. All these factors are part of economics.

Today's economists help businesses make decisions about how to use money. For instance, they might help a business decide how much money to spend on making products, paying employees, and investing in new equipment. Economists also help governments evaluate and improve economic conditions. Economics plays a key role in the management of households, businesses, and countries.

The first known writings about economics appeared about 400 B.C. in a book written by the Greek historian Xenophon (*ZEHN uh fuhn*). The title of the book, *Oeconomicus,* comes from the Greek words meaning "house" and "management." It is the root of the word *economics* used today.

Features of an Economy

▶ Tax Collection

The ancient Romans hired the first official tax collectors.

Throughout history, governments have carried out a wide range of responsibilities. They have protected the rights of citizens, managed relations with foreign countries, maintained military and police forces, and provided services for communities. To carry out their many tasks, governments have always needed to collect **taxes**—that is, money collected from individuals or businesses to fund the government.

The world's earliest governments developed among small groups of people. These governments had relatively few responsibilities, and their systems of taxation were simple. The systems were probably based on collecting and storing extra food for the community. By around 3500 B.C., villages were becoming small cities. As governments grew, they began to provide more services and direction for communities. As a result, their need for taxes grew.

Some governments helped organize their taxation systems by counting the number of people they ruled. The first known population counts were made thousands of years ago by the ancient Babylonians (people who lived in what is now southeastern Iraq), Chinese, and Egyptians. Such counts helped the government determine who owned land, who could pay taxes, and who could serve in the military.

Around 5 B.C., the **Roman** government hired people who were probably the first official tax collectors. These of-

Governments collect many types of taxes, but the most important are property taxes, **income** taxes, and transaction taxes. Property taxes are taxes people pay on the land they own. Income taxes are charged on the money earned by individuals or businesses. Transaction taxes are charged on various types of business activities, such as when goods are imported (brought in from a foreign country) or sold.

ficials registered all the citizens in an area, evaluated the value of their property, and collected taxes.

Today, governments in every country collect various types of taxes. Taxes give governments the money they need to build roads, operate public schools, manage park systems, and provide other services. Taxes help fund hospitals, police forces, and even the rockets that carry people into outer space.

Taxes fund police forces and other government services.

Features of an Economy

▶ Minted Coins

Clay tokens were used as money in the ancient past.

Some people traded beads before coins were invented.

The exchange of goods is important for every economy. Today, we use money to pay for the things people sell or the work they do. But early people did not have such a thing as money. Instead, they made purchases by exchanging objects, such as animal skins or tools. People soon found that certain goods would be accepted in trade (the buying and selling of goods) by almost everyone. These items included cloth, salt, cattle, and gold and silver objects. Gradually, people began to use these items in the same way that we use money today.

The first money took the form of beads, cacao beans (a type of evergreen seed), salt, shells, and other items. Metals like copper, silver, and gold were also used as money. Money simplified trade because everyone would accept it. Buyers no longer had to find particular items that were acceptable to trade for the goods they wanted. Money also made it easier for people to store wealth. A long-lasting pile of metal is easier to store than a pile of sugar or a horse.

Early metal coins had to be weighed every time they were used. A coin's worth depended on its weight, because coins were all slightly different sizes. This changed around the 600's B.C. in Lydia, an area that is now part of the country Turkey.

were also invented in ancient China and India. In China, people used knives, spades, and other metal tools for trade. About 1100 B.C., they began to use miniature bronze tools instead of real ones. Eventually, coins replaced the miniature tools.

In most countries today, only the government is allowed to mint coins. Although most of the money used today is paper **currency,** coins allow paper dollars to be divided into smaller amounts.

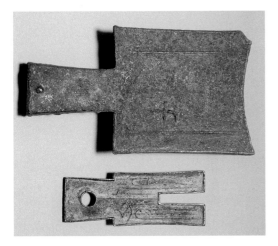

Long ago, some people used spades and other metal tools as money.

The people of Lydia made the first **minted coins.** Minted coins are made according to a standard pattern. Lydia's bean-shaped coins were made of a mixture of gold and silver. A stamp showed that the king of Lydia had guaranteed their value. With the arrival of minted coins, people no longer had to weigh coins to determine their value.

Many historians believe that coins

A CLOSER LOOK

Coins were first minted in America in 1652, in the Massachusetts Bay Colony. At the time, money was scarce because England did not provide the colonists with coins. English law said that only the king or queen of England could issue coins. The Massachusetts Bay Colony dated all the coins 1652, no matter when they were made. This helped the colonists get around the law, because England had no king or queen in 1652.

Features of an Economy

▶ Banks

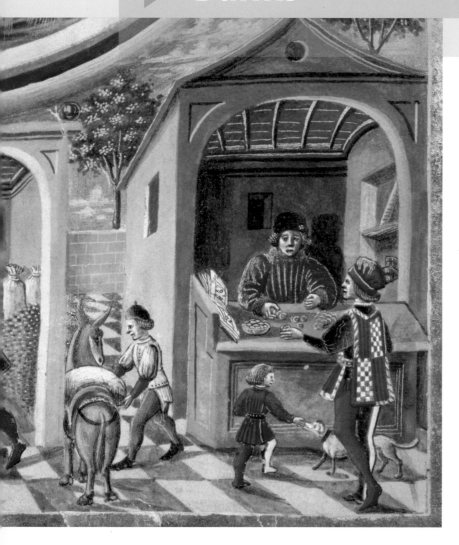

Early bankers worked from benches at the side of the street.

One of the world's most important economic advances was the development of the modern banking system. A **bank** is a business that accepts money from people and uses some of that money for loans and **investments.** Banks help money to flow more easily through the economy.

The first banking system was probably developed by the ancient **Romans** to support their trade network. But modern banking had its real beginnings in Italy during the 1200's. The word *bank* comes from the Italian word *banco*, which means "bench." Early Italian bankers worked from benches at the side of the street. Later, large banks were established in Rome, Venice, and other Italian cities. Banking soon began to spread through Europe.

By the 1600's, banks in London had developed many features similar to those of banks today. They paid **interest** to people who **deposited** money. Interest is a fee paid for the use of money. The banks then loaned out some of the deposited money to earn interest **income** for the bank. Individuals and businesses could make payments using written **drafts.** Such drafts are notes to the bank that an amount of money should be paid to a person. They are similar to modern **checks.**

Money deposited in today's banks is relatively safe, because most governments protect people from losing their deposits if the bank fails. Money can be withdrawn easily because banks keep cash available for their customers' needs. Deposited money earns interest, so it increases in value even while it is safely stored.

Today's banks encourage economic growth by providing a number of different services. They provide people with convenient ways to make payments, through services such as **checking accounts,** money transfers, online banking, and automatic bill payments. Many banks offer **credit cards,** which people use to charge purchases to an account that they must pay later. Banks also offer **debit cards,** which allow people to charge purchases to their checking account.

Another way that banks contribute to economic growth is by lending money to businesses and individuals. Businesses can borrow money to buy equipment or to invest in a new building. Individuals can borrow money to make large purchases, such as a house or car. Loans can promote the production and sale of goods, which helps to create more jobs.

Banks provide a safe place for people to keep their money.

Features of an Economy

▶ Paper Money

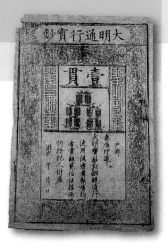

In ancient China, people used money made from tree bark.

Paper money was invented in China around A.D. 600.

The invention of paper **currency** made buying and selling goods easier. Paper currency was easier to carry and use than heavy coins. Although the paper itself was not valuable, paper money worked if everyone accepted it as payment. Most of the money used in the world today is made of paper.

The first paper money was developed in China, probably during the A.D. 600's. News of paper money reached Europe in the 1200's, after the Italian trader Marco Polo traveled to China. However, Europeans did not adopt paper currency until much later.

In the 1600's, European **banks** began to issue paper **bank notes.**

Such notes were receipts for money that could be exchanged for coins at the bank. Bank notes made up most of the paper bills in use until the 1800's.

The United States government printed its first paper money to help finance the American Revolution (1775-1783). As expenses increased, the U.S. government printed more and more money, called continentals. Eventually, the government printed so many continentals that the bills became practically worthless. As a result of these early problems, the United States stopped the widespread use of paper money until the 1860's.

The Federal Reserve System divides the United States into 12 banking districts.

In the early 1800's, many people in the United States would not accept bank notes as payment, because not every bank would exchange their notes for the stated value. When the U.S. government resumed printing paper money in the 1860's, people again did not trust the money's worth. The value of the new bills went up and down, just as the value of bank notes did. Finally, the government announced that it would pay gold coins for government bills.

The United States continued to have problems with its currency until 1913. At that time, Congress passed the Federal Reserve Act. This law created a central banking system still in use today. This system is called the Federal Reserve System. The Federal Reserve System helps to manage the economy by influencing the availability of money and loans.

Continentals were the first paper money in the United States. Today, the dollar is the most trusted currency in the world.

Features of an Economy

▶ Checks

People write checks to transfer money from bank accounts.

For thousands of years, buyers and sellers have invented new ways to simplify business activity. The invention of coins and paper money made buying and selling easier. The invention of **banks** helped people to keep their money safe from theft and loss. In the 1600's, London bankers developed another financial tool. Instead of withdrawing cash for every purchase, businesses and individuals could make payments using written **drafts** on their **bank accounts.** These drafts were the forerunner of today's **checks.**

A check is a written order telling a bank to transfer money from a **checking account** to a particular person or organization. Anyone who has money in a checking account can write a check. The person or organization receiving the money is called the payee. The payee can exchange the check for cash, which is called "cashing" the check. The payee can also **deposit** the check into a bank account or transfer it to another person or organization. The payee begins by endorsing the check, or signing it on the back. The payee then gives the check to the bank. The bank sends the money wherever the payee directs.

Checks are often more convenient to use than cash. Also, because only the listed payee can cash the check, checks are safer.

When a bank cashes or deposits a check from another bank, it collects the money by returning the check to the bank of the check writer. Sometimes the check is sent to a **clearinghouse.** Banks use clearinghouses to exchange checks and to determine how much the different banks owe one another. The first clearinghouse was established in London during the late 1700's. In 1853, the first U.S. clearinghouse was formed by New York City banks.

Today, **electronic banking** has made the use of checks less common.

Many people now use online banking, **debit cards,** and **electronic** payments rather than checks. However, checks remain the main method of payment in many parts of the world.

Today, electronic banking has reduced the use of checks.

Features of an Economy

▶ Stock Markets

As businesses grow, they sometimes need additional money to pay for new buildings, equipment, or other improvements. These **investments** will help make the business more **profitable** in the future. But how do businesses get this additional money? One way is by selling shares of **stock. Investors** who own a business's stock own a small portion of that business.

When individuals purchase a company's stock, they have the right to a share of the company's profit.

The New York Stock Exchange was established in 1792.

Stock can be bought and sold in a **stock exchange.** A stock exchange is a market where **brokers** help investors to buy and sell stocks. Stocks' values increase or decrease on the market depending on how the company is doing. If the company is doing well, stockholders might be able to sell their stock for a price higher than what they paid for it, thus making a profit. If the company is doing poorly, they might lose money when they sell their stock.

Initially, people who wanted to invest in a company had to find independent brokers. In 1531, the first European stock exchange was established in Antwerp, Belgium. Brokers gathered in a single location to buy and sell for their clients. London brokers gathered in coffee houses until they formed the first stock exchange in England in 1773. In New York City, brokers met under a Wall Street buttonwood tree until 1792, when they established the New York Stock Exchange. The stock exchange system makes it easier for individuals to invest in large corporations.

In 1881, stock exchanges were little more than noisy halls where brokers gathered.

Today, stock exchanges rely on electronics, but brokers still bustle around the noisy floor.

Today, there are major stock exchanges in such cities as New York, Chicago, London, and Tokyo. Investors trade billions of shares worth hundreds of billions of dollars every year.

These investments make money available to businesses and governments. This money, in turn, helps businesses and governments provide goods and services.

FUN FACT

Stock prices often reflect the state of a country's economy. If business conditions are good, stock prices usually rise, creating what is called a "bull market." If business conditions are poor, stock prices drop, causing a "bear market."

Features of an Economy

▶ Insurance

Insurance can cover many types of personal possessions, including cars and homes.

Another important development in economics was **insurance.** Insurance helps protect people and businesses from large losses of money in the case of certain events. For example, life insurance helps replace **income** lost to a family if a **wage**-earning parent dies. Health insurance helps pay medical bills. Fire insurance pays all or part of the loss if a homeowner's house is destroyed by fire.

People who want to be insured agree to make regular payments of money, called premiums, to an insur-ance company. In return, the company promises to repay them for certain losses. People buy insurance because they are willing to pay a relatively small amount of money in order to protect themselves against the chance of a disastrous loss.

The idea of insurance is thousands of years old. In the 1700's B.C., a form of insurance appeared in the Code of Hammurabi. This code is one of the earliest written collections of laws. It said that a borrower would not have to repay a loan if some personal misfortune made repayment impossible. For this protection, the borrower had to pay an extra amount in addition to the normal **interest.**

Around 1690, a London coffee house owned by Edward Lloyd was a popular

The Code of Hammurabi was written on a stone slab in the 1700's B.C.

meeting place for merchants (people who buy and sell goods) and ship owners. At this coffee house, people invented a practice called underwriting, which involved promising to help pay for something if it is lost. Under this system of underwriting, a ship's owner would create and post a list of the ship's cargo (load of goods). Anyone willing to share the risk of insuring the cargo would sign under the statement, indicating the amount of risk they were willing to guarantee in case of loss.

The coffee house eventually became Lloyd's of London (now Lloyd's), an insurance company famous for insuring almost any type of

risk. Lloyd's was the first company to offer many types of insurance that are common today. These types include insurance against burglary, hurricanes, and earthquakes.

Lloyd's coffee house in London helped bring about modern insurance.

Hammurabi

Hammurabi (?-1750 B.C.) was a Babylonian king who ruled from 1792 to 1750 B.C. During this time, he grew his kingdom into the great Babylonian Empire. Hammurabi is famous for assembling the Code of Hammurabi, one of the first written collections of laws. The code was based on older law collections, which Hammurabi revised and expanded. In the code, he promised to treat conquered peoples with justice and honor for their gods. The code covered many legal matters, such as false accusations, witchcraft, family laws, loans, and military service. The Code of Hammurabi was unearthed in 1901 and 1902, in southwestern Iran.

Features of an Economy

The vault in Fort Knox, Kentucky, holds thousands of gold bars.

Paper money made business transactions easier, but it only worked as long as everyone agreed on its worth. Early paper money created by the U.S. government became practically worthless when too much was printed. The problem was that the paper itself had no generally accepted value.

Gold, on the other hand, has been valuable for thousands of years. No one knows when gold was first discovered. **Archaeologists** have found gold jewelry near Varna, Bulgaria, dating back to about 4000 B.C. Gold coins were **minted** in Lydia during the 500's B.C.

Eventually, the **gold standard** was developed to take advantage of gold's generally accepted value. The gold standard uses gold as a "measuring stick" to determine the value of money. A country on the gold standard does two things. First, it agrees to exchange its money for a specific amount of gold. Second, it agrees to buy and sell gold at a fixed (set) price.

FUN FACT The governments of the world have about 42,000 tons (38 million kilograms) of gold. This gold is usually stored in brick-sized bars called ingots.

The gold standard gives people confidence in a **currency's** value. It also helps control government spending and limits **inflation.** Inflation happens when prices rise because there is too much money in circulation. In addition, the gold standard stabilizes exchange rates (the worth of one currency in relation to another) among countries that use it.

In 1695, the United Kingdom became the first country to adopt the gold standard. By the late 1800's, many other countries had followed suit.

During the 1860's, the U.S. government issued legal tender notes, or greenbacks, to help pay for the American Civil War (1861-1865). The government declared the money **legal tender,** which meant that people were required to accept it as payment. However, the greenback's value depended on people's confidence in the government. At one time, it decreased to 35 cents' worth of gold coin.

In 1879, the U.S. government announced that it would pay gold for greenbacks. This put the country on an unofficial gold standard. However, the move also meant that the federal government had no way to increase the supply of money when it needed to. The problem came to a climax during the 1896 presidential election,

when one party favored the gold standard and the other wanted to put more money into circulation. William McKinley, a member of the Republican Party who supported the gold standard, won the election.

The U.S. government stayed on the gold standard through the early 1900's. However, gold has played a smaller and smaller role in economies since the 1930's. The United States finally abandoned the gold standard in 1971.

Until 1971, U.S. currency was tied to the worth of gold.

Features of an Economy

▶ Labor Unions

U.S. Senator Hillary Rodham Clinton speaks to a federation of labor unions in 2008.

Both workers and businesses are essential to a healthy economy. Businesses need workers to produce the goods and services they sell, and workers need businesses to provide jobs. Workers also use their **income** to buy the goods and services that businesses offer. Workers and businesses need one another to be successful. However, they often have disagreements over pay, working conditions, and other issues.

The development of **labor unions** provided a way for workers and businesses to settle their disagreements. A trade union, or union, is an association of workers in a particular field. The purpose of the union is to promote and protect the workers' interests.

Many historians believe that the first true unions were formed in Europe during the **Industrial Revolution** of the late 1700's and early 1800's. During this period, the development of new machinery and factories transformed the way goods were produced. Soon, only the wealthy could afford the expensive machinery

When unions first developed in the United States, strikes often ended in violent confrontations.

Unions helped win shorter workdays, higher wages, and improvements in working conditions.

needed to run a business. These developments gave businesses a great deal of power. Individual workers had almost no say about their **wages,** working conditions, or the number of hours they had to work. Workers who complained were simply fired and replaced. The number of people competing for jobs forced the poor to work under horrible conditions.

Workers realized that they needed to organize into groups if they wanted businesses to listen to their complaints. If all the employees of a factory quit at once, the factory would have difficulty replacing everyone, be unable to produce goods at its usual pace, and lose money. As a result, the arrival of unions gave employers a strong reason to cooperate with workers' demands.

When the first unions developed in the United States during the mid-1800's, they faced strong opposition. Factory owners hired armed guards to crush strikes (an organized stopping of work). Many states passed laws that restricted or outlawed union activity.

Despite these setbacks, unions kept growing. Ultimately, they were able to win significant improvements, such as better working conditions, shorter hours, and higher wages. They helped bring about laws that forbade businesses from using young children as workers. They have also fought for workers' benefits, such as paid vacation time and health care. Labor unions continue their efforts to help workers throughout the world today.

Unions go on strike to put pressure on employers.

Features of an Economy

▶ Mail-Order Businesses

In 1872, a young American traveling salesman named Aaron Montgomery Ward came up with a new approach to selling goods. Along with his partner, George R. Thorne, Ward decided that he would buy large amounts of goods from manufacturers and then sell them directly to farmers through the mail. His business, Montgomery Ward and Company of Chicago, became wildly successful, paving the way for numerous **mail-order businesses** that followed.

Montgomery Ward and Company of Chicago was the first mail-order business to sell general merchandise (goods). Other mail-order businesses of the 1870's were merchants who sold only specialty goods.

In 1886, another mail-order business was launched by Richard W. Sears, a railroad station agent who sold watches by mail from Minnesota. After moving to Chicago, Sears became partners with Alvah C. Roebuck. The two men founded Sears, Roebuck and Co. in 1893. The company sold a wide

Montgomery Ward made a variety of goods available to farmers.

"A BUSY BEE-HIVE."
SECTIONAL VIEW OF THE ENORMOUS ESTABLISHMENT OF
MONTGOMERY WARD & CO.
MICHIGAN AVENUE, MADISON AND WASHINGTON STREETS, CHICAGO.

Aaron Montgomery Ward

Aaron Montgomery Ward (1844-1913) was an American businessman who pioneered mail-order business in the United States. After working as a traveling salesman in the Midwest, he started a mail-order business with his partner, George R. Thorne. They began the business with $2,400 and a single-sheet catalog listing a few dry goods items. When Ward died in 1913, their stream of **income** had risen to $40 million per year.

variety of products. By the early 1900's, it was the largest mail-order company in the world.

Mail-order companies initially served customers who lived on farms or in small towns. But after World War I (1914-1918), improved roads and the increased use of cars made it easier for people to shop in larger towns and cities. As a result, mail-order sales declined. Some mail-order firms, such as the Sears company, reached customers by opening stores in towns and cities.

After World War II (1939-1945), mail-order businesses developed new methods of reaching customers in rapidly growing cities and towns. The **in-dustry** soon began to grow again.

Today, the traditional mail-order business is often called the direct-marketing business, because of the many methods used to reach customers. Mail-order businesses advertise through magazines, newspapers, radio, television, telephone, and the **Internet.** Companies use Web sites to reach customers worldwide.

Mail-order businesses declined as it became easier for people to travel to shopping centers.

Features of an Economy

▶ Credit Cards

Customers can use credit cards by swiping them in special machines.

Credit is the ability to purchase goods or services even if someone does not immediately have enough money to pay. This ability enables people to buy more goods, which in turn causes businesses to hire more workers to produce those goods. At the same time, businesses can use credit to purchase new equipment that will help them increase production over time. For these reasons, credit can help promote economic growth and contribute to a nation's wealth.

In the late 1920's, the introduction of the **credit card** in the United States made it easier for people to buy things using credit. A credit card is a small card that identifies the owner, usually by a printed name and signature. It allows its owner to charge purchases to a **bank account.** Charged purchases are recorded and can be paid later. The first credit cards were issued by individual companies, such as hotels, department stores, restaurants, and fuel companies. These cards could be used for purchases only from the company that offered the card.

In 1950, the Diner's Club, Inc., introduced the first "travel and entertainment card." The American Express Company issued another card in 1958. These credit cards could be used at many different businesses. They charged cardholders a yearly fee and billed them for purchases on a regular schedule, usually monthly. Merchants who accepted the card paid a service charge to the card company, usually between 4 and 7 percent of the amounts charged.

Around the same time, another type of credit card system was introduced: the bank credit card system. When a person charged a purchase to a bank credit card, the **bank** paid money to the merchant's account as soon as it received a record of the charge. The bank recorded the individual's charges and provided a bill for the total on a regular schedule. The cardholder could either pay the full amount or make monthly **installment** payments. People who chose to pay their accounts over time had to pay **interest** on the balance due.

Today, credit cards are issued by many different types of businesses and are accepted almost everywhere. Cardholders simply present the card when they wish to make a purchase. They are billed monthly for what they spend. Cards usually allow cardholders to pay the balance due over time, with interest or finance charges added.

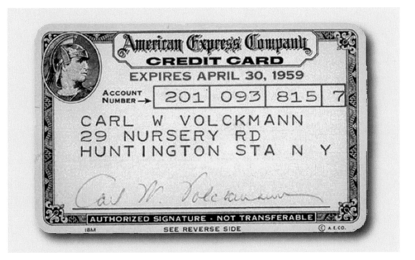

American Express began to offer credit cards in 1958.

Cardholders are billed monthly for their credit card purchases.

Features of an Economy

▶ The Bar Code

In 1879, an American restaurant owner named James Ritty invented a machine that would come to be used by many businesses: the mechanical cash register. The cash register could add up purchases quickly and accurately.

By the end of the 1800's, cash registers had a drawer that stored cash. Every time the register's cash drawer opened, a bell rang, which helped to reduce theft. Later cash registers could also print out the amount of money received with each sale. This allowed store managers to compare the cash register record with

Cash registers required clerks to enter the price of purchased goods by hand.

the money in the cash drawer, to make sure the amounts matched. The cash register was the starting point for a number of technological improvements that greatly improved business sales and record-keeping.

About 100 years after the cash register was first used, a new invention emerged: the **bar code.** A bar code is a pattern of printed bars that a computer can translate into information. It also includes a line of numbers or other characters that represent the same information as the bars. When bar codes are placed on items for sale,

A bar code is a pattern of printed bars that can be read by computers.

9 788679 912077

they enable **electronic** devices called scanners to identify the items instantly.

At a store's checkout counter, a scanner uses a **laser** beam to read an item's bar code. Sometimes the scanner is handheld. Other scanners are built into a counter, located beneath a small window. The scanner reads the bars as a series of numbers. The store computer uses the numbers to search a database of product information. The computer also records product sales, helping stores keep track of the amount of each item they have in stock (available for sale).

In 1973, the Universal Product Code (UPC) was adopted as the standard retail bar code system in the United States and Canada. UPC's first appeared on U.S. grocery store products in 1974. In 1976, the European Article Number (EAN) code was adopted as the bar code standard in Europe.

Today, there are several different types of bar code systems. The GS1 system uses bar codes based on unique identification numbers for store items. These numbers can be 8, 12, 13, or 14 digits long, but the most common system uses 13 digits.

Many businesses today have replaced cash registers with scanners connected to computer terminals. Bar codes have made it easier and faster to purchase many goods.

Handheld scanners read bar codes to help store owners keep track of their inventory.

Bar codes made purchasing groceries much quicker, while also reducing the chance for mistakes.

▶ The Automated Teller Machine

Money machines dispensed cash starting in the 1960's.

Beginning in the mid-1900's, a number of technological advances made it easier for individuals and businesses to manage money, purchases, and products. **Credit cards** enabled people to charge goods for later payment. **Bar codes** let stores track sales **electronically. Debit cards** allowed people to have purchase amounts deducted directly from their **checking accounts.** Another important ad-

vance was the introduction of the **automated teller machine (ATM).**

The automated teller machine is a computer terminal that operates as a miniature **bank** office. ATM's provide people with access to their **bank accounts** from a variety of locations, at all times of day and night. ATM's are sometimes called cash machines or cash dispensers, but they can do much more than simply dispense (give out) cash. They allow people to make banking transactions, such as **deposits** or transfers between accounts.

In order to use an ATM, a customer inserts a special plastic card that resembles a credit card. The card stores the customer's account information, which is coded in a magnetic stripe or a computer chip. After the

FUN FACT Automated teller machines first appeared in the early 1970's. By 2007, there were more than 415,000 ATM's in the United States.

card is inserted into the ATM, the customer enters a security code called a personal identification number (PIN). The machine uses the customer's account number to access the bank account. Then, the customer selects what the machine should do. Using a device called a vacuum pump or rubberized rollers, the machine can count and dispense paper money.

The first cash-dispensing machines were introduced in the late 1960's. These were the forerunners to the ATM. By the early 1970's, the more powerful ATM was in use. Today, ATM's can be found at banks, airports, stores, and shopping centers,

as well as at many other public locations. ATM's enable people to do banking at their convenience, and they give people much greater access to cash.

Banking once required meeting with a teller during the day.

ATM's read bank cards, giving customers access to 24-hour banking.

Features of an Economy

▶ Electronic Commerce

E-commerce allows people to pay bills without using checks.

The introduction of **checks** made buying and selling easier for customers and businesses. Starting in the late 1990's, **electronic commerce,** or e-commerce, made things even more convenient. E-commerce refers to the **electronic** exchange of money for goods and services. The introduction of the **World Wide Web** in the 1990's enabled companies to conduct business with customers and other businesses electronically over the **Internet.**

E-commerce includes a wide variety of online transactions. Business-to-business (B2B) transactions involve the use of the Internet or a private computer network to coordinate sales and deliveries between two or more businesses. Product orders, business communication, and billing are all handled electronically. Only the actual products are transported physically.

Another type of e-commerce is a business-to-consumer (B2C) transaction, which is a sale that a business makes directly to an individual. Many businesses have online "stores" on the World Wide Web. These stores are made up of computer files that may contain text, pictures, sounds, and video. Businesses that operate online stores can present customers with many more product choices than they could in a regular store. Some products, such as computer **software** and music, can even be delivered to customers electronically. Other types of products are physically delivered.

One popular form of e-commerce is the online auction. In these auctions, individuals and businesses offer items for sale, and online shoppers bid against one another to make a purchase. A company that hosts online auctions makes money by charging sellers a small fee, or by collecting a percentage of an item's selling price.

E-commerce allows buyers and sellers to share and compare product information more efficiently than they could in the past. It also allows buyers and sellers separated by distance or international borders to connect with one another.

Items purchased on the Internet are shipped directly to customers.

Economic Systems

▶ Feudalism

As societies have developed over time, the ways that economies are organized have changed greatly. In addition, people have sometimes deliberately altered the way economies work, usually in an effort to make them more efficient or fair. As the world grows toward a truly global economy, there is no doubt that economics will continue to develop.

Under feudalism, peasants paid taxes to nobles, who served the king.

During the **Middle Ages** (the period from about the 400's through the 1400's), land in western Europe was divided into many countries. In place of the central **Roman** government, which had ruled previously, different kings ruled with the support of nobles (members of the ruling **class**). In this environment, a new political, economic, and military system called **feudalism** began to develop.

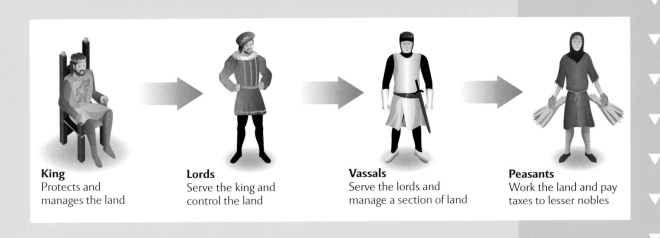

King
Protects and
manages the land

Lords
Serve the king and
control the land

Vassals
Serve the lords and
manage a section of land

Peasants
Work the land and pay
taxes to lesser nobles

Under feudalism, wealthy nobles who controlled land became known as lords. As lords, they divided the land into sections that were ruled by lesser nobles called vassals, who promised service to their lord. The lord, in turn, promised service to the king.

Most vassals did not own the land they controlled. However, they were entitled to whatever goods the land produced. A vassal collected **taxes,** held court to settle disagreements among people in his service, and kept a private army to defend his territory. The main service a vassal owed his lord was military. In exchange for claiming the output of the land, a vassal provided his lord with a certain number of warriors, usually only for a limited number of days.

Vassals also managed the peasants who worked the land. Peasants were almost completely at their vassal's mercy. The vassal decided their living conditions, taxes, rents, work, and various fees. Many peasants were serfs, who were said to be "bound to the soil." Even when the land changed rulers, the serfs remained to work their patch of land.

Feudalism helped provide some order during a time when Europe was experiencing frequent wars and disputes over land. It also provided a way to exchange goods and services after the Roman system had collapsed. Feudalism did not rely as much on money, because goods and services were often exchanged directly.

Despite its advantages, feudalism limited economic growth. As money came into wider use again in the 1200's, the feudal system began to dissolve. Still, aspects of feudalism formed much of the basis for modern governments in Europe.

In feudal systems, authority flowed downward from the king.

Economic Systems

▶ Mercantilism

Mercantilist countries aimed to export goods.

As **feudalism** disappeared, an economic system called **mercantilism** emerged in Europe. Mercantilism was based on the idea that countries should increase their wealth by exporting more than they imported. Exporting is selling goods to other countries. Importing is buying goods from other countries. Mercantilism thrived between the 1500's and 1700's.

Mercantile countries measured wealth only by the amount of gold and silver in their **treasuries.** To increase that wealth, they strictly regulated agriculture, **industry,** and trade. Mercantile countries discouraged imports by forcing buyers to pay high **taxes** on them. Such countries tried to develop resources and industries within their own borders, so that they would not need to import as many goods.

During the mid-1700's, a group of French economists opposed mercantilism. They supported the idea known as laissez faire (*LEHS ay FAIR*), which held that business and trade should be free from government regulation. They argued that high taxes on imported goods should be replaced with a single property tax.

The great Scottish economist Adam Smith also opposed mercantilism. Best known for his book *The Wealth of Nations* (1776), Smith argued for free trade and less government interference in the economy. Today, Smith is considered the founder of modern economics.

Three British economists helped build on Smith's ideas in the late 1700's and the 1800's. David Ricardo demonstrated the advantages of free trade among countries. Thomas Robert Malthus warned that

John Stuart Mill was an economist during the 1800's who favored a free-market system.

rapid population growth could lead to food shortages, disease, and wars. John Stuart Mill also supported the idea of the **free-market system.**

Adam Smith

Adam Smith (1723-1790) was born in Kirkcaldy, Scotland. He studied at the University of Glasgow and Oxford University. In 1751, he became a professor at Glasgow. Smith's 1759 work, *The Theory of Moral Sentiments*, earned him a tutoring position for the young French Duke of Buccleuch in 1764. He began writing *The Wealth of Nations* while in France. When he returned to England in 1766, he retired from teaching and devoted the next 10 years to writing. *The Wealth of Nations*, published in 1776, discussed economic processes and argued against the British mercantile system's restrictions on free trade.

Economic Systems

▶ Capitalism

Capitalism is an economic system in which individual households and businesses control the economy. Capitalism is also called the **free-market system,** because individuals are free to make their own economic decisions. The opposite of capitalism is central planning, a system in which the government controls the economy. In the real world, no economy uses pure capitalism or pure central planning. Every economy has features of both. But some countries, such as the United States and Canada, emphasize the free market enough that they can be considered capitalistic.

The free-market system was first proposed by Adam Smith in *The Wealth of Nations.* Smith believed that the government should let individual households and businesses pursue their own interests. He believed that individuals and businesses working for their own best interests would naturally benefit both society and the economy. Smith argued that countries would increase wealth most rapidly by allowing free trade.

Smith's ideal capitalistic economy would work through "pure competition." Businesses would provide goods and services for people to use, and individuals would decide which goods and services to buy. Businesses would need workers to make their goods and services, and individuals would decide how much time to

Adam Smith's writings were the foundation for modern economics.

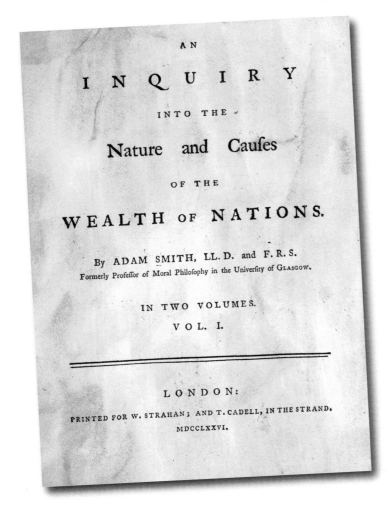

AN
INQUIRY
INTO THE
Nature and Caufes
OF THE
WEALTH OF NATIONS.

By ADAM SMITH, LL. D. and F. R. S.
Formerly Profeffor of Moral Philofophy in the Univerfity of GLASGOW.

IN TWO VOLUMES.
VOL. I.

LONDON:
PRINTED FOR W. STRAHAN; AND T. CADELL, IN THE STRAND.
MDCCLXXVI.

In the 1800's, London was the center of the capitalist world.

spend working. Businesses would need invested money to grow, and individuals would decide how much money to invest in businesses.

Under Smith's ideas, competition among businesses would help lower prices for goods and services. Competition among workers for jobs, along with competition among businesses for workers, would help determine how much people were paid. In theory, pure competition, with no government involvement, would lead to the perfect combination of goods, services, prices, **wages,** and employment.

In the real world, capitalism operates somewhat differently from Smith's theories. As a result, capitalistic governments take certain actions that affect the economy. For instance, they create laws to help ensure com-

petition and to protect the public. They also create programs to help people who need food, housing, or other basic necessities. In the real world, capitalism drives the economy, while governments strive to keep the economy stable.

Today, capitalism drives the global economy.

Economic Systems

▶ Communism

V. I. Lenin led the revolution in Russia in 1917.

In the late 1800's, the German philosopher Karl Marx opposed Adam Smith's view that free trade would lead to the greatest good for society. Instead, Marx argued that Smith's ideas would lead to economic **depressions** that would leave workers in bad conditions. Marx believed that human history had been a struggle between **classes** over resources. In place of **capitalism,** Marx proposed an economic system called **Communism.**

Communism is a political and economic system in which property is owned by the central government. In most Communist systems, the government owns and runs the "means of production"—that is, factories, land, and other resources. The government also plans the country's economic activity. Marx believed that Communism would eventually lead to the creation of a classless society, where all people would live in peace, prosperity, and freedom. He believed that people would no longer need governments, police, or the military.

During the early 1900's, the Russian revolutionary leader V. I. Lenin expanded upon Marx's ideas. He believed that political change would be led by a core group of revolutionaries, which he called the Communist Party. Lenin led a revolution that took control of Russia. In 1922, the Communist Party created the Union of Soviet Socialist Republics, commonly called the Soviet Union. Communism soon spread to many countries around the world.

Millions of people lived under Communist rule during the 1900's. Communist governments typically valued group needs over the needs of individuals, and they sought to control almost every aspect of people's lives. People living in Communist countries lost many personal freedoms. In addition, many Communist governments were violent and corrupt.

By the late 1970's, Communism appeared to be failing in many parts of the world. The Soviet Union broke apart in 1991, and Communists remained in power in only a small number of countries. Today, of the Communist countries that remain, many have introduced economic reforms to shift their economies toward capitalism.

Communist dictatorships sought to control every aspect of people's lives.

Das Kapital was one of Karl Marx's most famous works.

Karl Marx

Karl Marx (1818-1883) was one of the most important thinkers of the 1800's. He was born in the town of Trier, in what is now western Germany. He earned a philosophy degree from the University of Jena in 1841 and moved to Paris in 1843. There, Marx became friends with the German journalist Friedrich Engels. With Engels, he wrote the *Communist Manifesto* (1848). In 1849, Marx went to London. In London, Marx wrote his most ambitious work, *Das Kapital (Capital)*. Only the first volume was published during his lifetime, in 1867. Engels edited the second and third volumes after Marx died in 1883.

Economic Systems

▶ Globalization

Today, many corporations conduct business around the world.

Over the years, travel, trade, and the spread of culture have made the different nations of the world more closely connected. This trend, commonly called **globalization,** accelerated in the late 1900's, due in part to technological developments. These developments included improvements in communication, transportation, printing, shipping, and computer technology. Through globalization, individuals, groups, and organizations throughout the world have become more closely linked.

In economic terms, globalization represents an increasingly international approach to the production, distribution, and **marketing** of goods and services. Globalization involves an emphasis on international transactions and an increase in worldwide communication.

One of the main features of globalization has been the growth of multinational corporations (businesses that have branches and operations in many countries). Such corporations have greater flexibility and access to resources than corporations that operate in only one country. For example, if a multinational corporation's plant in one country is losing money, the corporation can close it down and move operations to another country. Such a move can give a company new opportunities to make greater **profits.**

Most countries in Europe are now members of the European Union.

Another major feature of globalization is the reduction and elimination of international trade restrictions, such as high **taxes** on imports (items brought in from a foreign country). Many countries belong to trade agreements like the General Agreement on Tariffs and Trade (GATT) and the North American Free Trade Agreement (NAFTA). Powerful international organizations, such as the World Trade Organization (WTO) and the World Bank, also develop economic policies and encourage global cooperation.

The development of the **European Union (EU)** was a major event in the trend toward globalization. Following World War II (1939-1945), a French statesman named Jean Monnet suggested that European countries should come together to improve their economies. Several countries of western Europe eventually cooperated in economic affairs as members of the European Community (EC). In 1992, the EC member countries created the EU and took steps to adopt a common **currency,** the euro. Today, most countries in Europe are members of the EU.

Economic globalization has been the subject of much debate. Many people believe that globalization will cause the world's economy to become more efficient and to grow more rapidly. They believe that globalization is a step toward a "global village" with increased understanding and cooperation worldwide.

Opponents of globalization argue that the trend favors powerful nations, gives too much power to corporate interests, treats workers unfairly, and interferes with the governments of individual countries.

Many companies hire people from around the world to work remotely.

1700's B.C. The Code of Hammurabi recorded an early form of insurance.

c. 1100 B.C. The Chinese began using miniature bronze tools as a medium of exchange.

600's B.C. The first minted coins were produced in Lydia.

c. 400 B.C. The Greek historian and author Xenophon wrote *Oeconomicus*.

c. 5 B.C. Roman census takers acted as early tax collectors.

A.D. 600's The first paper money was developed in China.

A.D. 700's Feudalism began to appear in Europe.

1200's Modern banking developed in Italy.

1531 The first European stock exchange was established in Antwerp, Belgium.

1500's The economic system of mercantilism became prominent in Europe.

1600's London bankers developed a system for making payments with written drafts, the forerunner of today's checks.

c. 1690 The process of underwriting was developed in London.

1700's The first true unions were formed during the Industrial Revolution.

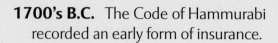

1773 The London Stock Exchange was established.

1776 Adam Smith's *The Wealth of Nations* was published.

1792 The New York Stock Exchange was established.

1848 Karl Marx's *Communist Manifesto* was published.

1872 Aaron Montgomery Ward developed his mail-order business.

1879 The U.S. government adopted an unofficial gold standard.

1879 James Ritty invented the cash register.

1917 The Communist Party gained control of Russia.

1920's The first credit cards were issued.

Early 1970's Automated teller machines (ATM's) were introduced.

1973 The Universal Product Code (UPC) was adopted as the standard retail bar code system in the United States and Canada.

1992 The European Union was established.

Late 1990's The Internet and the World Wide Web contributed greatly to economic globalization and the growth of electronic commerce.

▶ Glossary

archaeologist a person who studies the people, customs, and life of ancient times.

automated teller machine (ATM) a computer terminal that can operate as a miniature bank office, where people can perform a number of different banking transactions.

bank a financial firm that accepts people's deposits and uses them to make loans and investments.

bank account the money in a bank that can be withdrawn by a depositor; a checking, savings, or other account with a bank.

bank note a paper note that could be exchanged for coins at a bank.

bar code a pattern of lines and bars that a computer can translate into information about an item.

broker a person who buys and sells stocks, bonds, or other commodities for other people.

capitalism an economic model that calls for control of the economy by individual households and privately owned businesses.

check a written order directing a bank to pay money to a person or organization.

checking account a bank account against which bank checks may be drawn at any time.

class a group of people who share a common status or position in society.

clearinghouse an institution used by banks to exchange checks and to establish claims against each other that result from financial transactions.

Communism a political and economic system in which property is owned by the central government.

credit card a card that allows people to charge purchases to an account that they must pay later.

currency money in use in a country.

debit card a card that allows people to charge purchases to a checking account.

deposit (n.) money paid as a pledge to do something or to pay more later; money placed in a bank for safekeeping; (v.) to put in a place to be kept safe.

depression a deep, extended slump in total business activity.

draft a written order directing the payment of a certain amount of money.

electronic of or having to do with electrons.

electronic banking banking with computers and other electronic equipment.

electronic commerce the electronic exchange of money for goods and services.

European Union (EU) an organization of European countries that works for cooperation among its members.

feudalism the political, economic, and military system of western Europe during the Middle Ages. Under this system, people gave military and other services to a person of higher rank, in return for protection and the use of land.

free-market system an economic system in which individuals are free to make their own decisions.

globalization the trend toward increased economic, cultural, and social connectedness across international borders.

gold standard the use of gold as the standard of value for the money of a country.

income money that comes in from business or work.

Industrial Revolution a period in the late 1700's and early 1800's when the development of industries brought great change to many parts of the world.

industry any branch of business, trade, or manufacture.

inflation a continual increase in prices throughout a nation's economy.

insurance a way of providing protection against financial loss in the case of certain events.

installment a part of a sum of money or of a debt to be paid at stated times.

interest the price paid to lenders for the use of their money.

Internet a vast network of computers that connects many of the world's businesses, institutions, and individuals.

investment the use of savings to produce future income. Direct investments involve investing in a business or property. Indirect investments involve putting money in savings accounts or buying stocks or bonds.

investor a person who uses money to buy something that will produce a profit, or an income, or both.

labor union an organization that brings together workers to promote better job conditions.

laser a device that produces an intense, focused beam of light.

legal tender any type of money that must, by law, be accepted in payment of a debt.

mail-order business a business involving the sale of products by mail.

marketing the process by which sellers and buyers find each other.

mercantilism an economic system followed by England, France, and other nations from the 1500's to the late 1700's. Under this system, a nation's government strictly regulated economic affairs.

Middle Ages the period in European history between ancient and modern times, from about the A.D. 400's through the 1400's.

minted coin money that is coined by public authority.

profit; profitable the money that is left when the cost of goods and of carrying on business is subtracted from the amount of money taken in; yielding a financial profit.

Roman of or having to do with ancient Rome or its people. The Roman Empire controlled most of Europe and the Middle East from 27 B.C. to A.D. 476.

salary fixed pay for regular work.

software the designs, instructions, routines, and other printed matter required for the operation of a computer or other automatic machine.

stock a right of ownership in a corporation. Stock is divided into a certain number of shares.

stock exchange a marketplace where brokers act as agents for the public in buying and selling stocks and bonds.

tax money collected from individuals or businesses to fund the government.

treasury the department of a government or organization that has charge of the income and expenses of a country.

wage the price paid for work.

World Wide Web a vast system of computer files linked together on the Internet.

Books:

- *Amazing Leonardo da Vinci Inventions You Can Build Yourself* by Maxine Anderson (Nomad Press, 2006).

- *Economics: Today and Tomorrow* (Student Edition) (McGraw-Hill, 2007).

- *From Seashells to Smart Cards: Money and Currency* by Ernestine Giesecke & Daniel Condon (Heinemann Library, 2003).

- *Great Inventions: The Illustrated Science Encyclopedia* by Peter Harrison, Chris Oxlade, and Stephen Bennington (Southwater Publishing, 2001).

- *Great Inventions of the 20th Century* by Peter Jedicke (Chelsea House Publications, 2007).

- *How to Enter and Win an Invention Contest* by Edwin J. Sobey (Enslow, 1999).

- *Inventions* by Valerie Wyatt (Kids Can Press, 2003).

- *So You Want to Be an Inventor?* By Judith St. George (Philomel Books, 2002).

- *What a Great Idea! Inventions that Changed the World* by Stephen M. Tomecek (Scholastic, 2003).

Web Sites:

- A Comparative Chronology of Money from Ancient Times to Present Day
  http://www.ex.ac.uk/~RDavies/arian/amser/chrono.html
  This site, based on a book by Glyn Davies, emeritus professor of economics at the University of Wales, traces the history of money from 9000 B.C. to the 21st century.

- H.I.P. Pocket Change for Kids
  http://www.usmint.gov/kids
  The U.S. Mint's official Web site for students includes games, cartoons, and information about the U.S. Mint.

- Exploring Leonardo - Museum of Science, Boston
  http://www.mos.org/sln/Leonardo
  Focusing on Leonardo da Vinci, this is a useful site for teachers and students in grades 4-8. Areas covered include a helpful section on the elements of machines (the lever, gears), and a discussion of perspective.

- Inventor of the Week
  http://web.mit.edu/invent/iow/i-archive-cp.html
  The Lemelson-MIT program's Web site includes an index searchable by invention or inventor, games and trivia, and links to other sources.

- Kids Pages - United States Patent and Trademark Office
  http://www.uspto.gov/go/kids
  The U.S. Patent and Trademark Office's student Web site includes games, puzzles, links to information about inventions, and a glossary.

- National Inventors Hall of Fame
  http://www.invent.org/index.asp
  Information on inventions and inventors from the National Inventors Hall of Fame.